This Book Belongs to

The mission of Storey Communications is to serve our customers by publishing practical information that encourages personal independence in harmony with the environment.

Edited by Pamela Lappies
Cover and interior illustrations by Mary Rich
Design and production by Meredith Maker
Production assistance by Susan Bernier
Indexed by Northwind Editorial Services

Some recipes have been adapted from other Storey/Garden Way Publishing books: pages 10, 52: *The Joy of Gardening Cookbook* by Janet Ballantyne; pages 7, 38: *Herbal Treasures* by Phyllis V. Shaudys; page 20: *Weekend!* by Edith Stovel and Pamela Wakefield; pages 26, 34, 40: *Making Quick Breads* by Barbara Karoff; and page 48: *The Bread Book* by Ellen Foscue Johnson.

The information in this book is true and complete to the best of our knowledge. All recommendations are made without guarantee on the part of the author or

Storey Communications, Inc. The author and publisher disclaim any liability in connection with the use of this information. For additional information please contact Storey Communications, Inc., Schoolhouse Road, Pownal, Vermont 05261.

Printed in Canada by Métropole Litho

10 9 8 7 6 5 4 3 2 1

**Library of Congress
Cataloging-in-Publication Data**

Bass, Ruth, 1934–
    Herbal breads / Ruth Bass.
        p.   cm.
    "A fresh-from-the-garden cookbook."
    "A Storey Publishing Book."
    ISBN 0-88266-923-0 (hc : alk paper)
    1. Cookery (Herbs)   2. Bread.
      I. Title.
TX819.H4B38 1996
641.8'15—dc20   96-1720
                          CIP

HeRBAL BReADs

A
Fresh from the Garden
Cookbook

RUTH BASS

ILLUSTRATED BY MARY RICH

STOREY

A Storey Publishing Book
Storey Communications, Inc.

Introduction

My grandmother made two loaves of white bread every day for her family and went to bed each night knowing that it was all gone, and she'd have to start over in the morning. She had, eventually, eleven children, so a couple of loaves of bread didn't last long. My mother made bread, too, but not as often. Hers didn't last either. It was usually oatmeal, and we could smell that bread reaching the baked stage from several rooms away. We'd be on hand when the crusty loaves came out of the oven, teasing to have it cut so we could slather on butter, watch it melt, and eat the bread warm.

My mother always resisted, telling us the same thing every time. "It ruins the loaf to cut it when it's hot." And then she'd give in. At our house now, we don't even pretend to worry about crushing loaves — we just slice it hot and let the butter melt.

Making bread is addictive. The satisfaction is enormous, not only from the actual achievement but from the accolades that envelop you as people bite into hot muffins, beautiful biscuits, or a tall loaf of herb bread.

In addition, if it's a bread made with yeast, you get to knead. People who teach stress management ought to introduce breadmaking into their courses. A few 10-minute sessions of pummeling that resistant dough and most tensions have tucked themselves right into that fat, resistant elasticity that is going to be bread. No wonder Grandma never missed her breadmaking.

Yeast bread, outside of a bread machine, does require the cook's attendance.

You have to mix it, knead it, let it rise an hour or more, punch it, knead it, let it rise again, and bake it. It's not something to be tackled when you're going to the dentist or having lunch out. On those days, make muffins, tortillas, the aptly named quick breads, pancakes, or dumplings. Herbs find themselves right at home in all these places, too.

Here are a few hints gathered from grandmothers, mothers, friends, and the flour itself:

1. Use fresh herbs whenever the recipe says "dried." Try twice as much at first and then tone it down — or up — the second time around to suit your own palate.
2. Always wash store-bought herbs. If you're going to mince them anyway, squeeze them inside a paper towel. It's hard to chop wet herbs finely.
3. For breads, mince the herbs very fine. You're looking for taste, not texture.
4. Substitute tarragon for basil, rosemary for savory, thyme for oregano, and see what you think. Pairing them is like marriage: sometimes it works, sometimes it doesn't.
5. Get rid of those tough stems on the fresh herbs. Sometimes you can just pull the stem through your thumb and forefinger, down from the top. Or scrape the leaves off with a knife on a board.

6. For the sometimes sticky quick breads, put a piece of wax paper into the bottom of the pan after the sides and bottom have been greased. You'll have fewer broken corners.
7. Bake in different shapes. Lots of breads will cook beautifully in a coffee can, in a round or square casserole, or on a cookie sheet.
8. If you live in a house where bread doesn't feel toasty enough to rise, get out the heating pad. It will cure sluggish dough even quicker than it fixes up your aching back. Put the pad under the bowl, and turn it on low until you get a feeling for how much heat you need. It works.
9. Remember that flour has personality. Sometimes it has a mind of its own. It is not scientific, so a second loaf may not be exactly like the first, even from a precise instrument like a bread machine. If you're mixing and kneading, you may use 4 cups of flour one time, 4½ the next. Just make it feel right.

Thyme and Cheese Biscuits

Wheat, herbs, and cheese cause a major personality change in old-fashioned baking powder biscuits. Other herbs can be substituted for the ones here.

½ cup whole wheat flour
1½ cups unbleached all-purpose flour
3 teaspoons baking powder
1 teaspoon minced fresh thyme
½ teaspoon minced fresh parsley
½ teaspoon minced fresh rosemary
½ cup shredded Monterey Jack cheese
5 tablespoons butter
½ cup milk, possibly more

1. Preheat the oven to 450°F. Grease a cookie sheet and set aside. Mix flours, baking powder, herbs, and cheese in a large mixing bowl, using a fork. Cut in the butter. The mixture will be crumbly.
2. Add the milk and stir until the ingredients hold together. More milk may be needed.
3. Drop large spoonfuls of the sticky dough on the cookie sheet at least an inch apart. Bake 10–12 minutes or until a toothpick inserted in the center comes out clean.

1 DOZEN BISCUITS

Apple Muffins

Almost any fruit can be added to a muffin, and most of them have been — cranberries, raisins, peaches, strawberries, blueberries. Apples are a happy choice, too, as long as they are finely chopped.

1 cup unbleached all-purpose flour
½ cup whole wheat flour
⅓ cup sugar
2 teaspoons baking powder
½ teaspoon salt
¼ cup powdered buttermilk
½ teaspoon nutmeg
2 teaspoons minced fresh sage
4 tablespoons butter, softened
1 egg
¾ cup water
2 medium apples, finely chopped (1 cup)
½ teaspoon cinnamon
⅓ cup dark brown sugar

1. Preheat the oven to 375°F. Grease a muffin tin and set aside. In a large bowl, combine the two kinds of flour, sugar, baking powder, salt, buttermilk, nutmeg, and sage.
2. Add the butter, egg, water, and apple and mix quickly. Fill the muffin cups about two-thirds full. Mix the cinnamon and brown sugar and sprinkle on each muffin.
3. Bake for 20 minutes.

1 DOZEN MUFFINS

Sweet Potato Muffins

Sweet potatoes create a mellow, yellow muffin. This one has herbs for flavor and some zucchini for volume.

1½ cups unbleached all-purpose flour
¼ cup sugar
½ teaspoon baking powder
2 teaspoons baking soda
½ teaspoon salt
½ cup vegetable oil
½ cup brown sugar
2 eggs
1 teaspoon vanilla extract
¾ pounds sweet potatoes, cooked and mashed (1½ cups)
¾ pounds unpeeled zucchini, shredded (1½ cups)
1 tablespoon minced fresh tarragon
1½ teaspoons cinnamon

1. Preheat the oven to 375°F. Grease 2 muffin tins or line with paper muffin cups. Sift together the flour, sugar, baking powder, baking soda, and salt. In a separate large bowl, beat the oil, brown sugar, eggs, and vanilla.
2. Stir the sweet potatoes, zucchini, tarragon, and cinnamon into the oil and egg mixture. Add the flour mixture and stir until blended.
3. Pour the batter into the muffin tins. Bake for 20 minutes.

2 DOZEN REGULAR SIZE MUFFINS OR 1 DOZEN OVERSIZE MUFFINS

Aromatic Pancakes

Some brunches are breakfast. Some brunches are lunch. Pancakes with fruit and herbs create a tasty bridge between the two and are a perfect brunch offering. The adventurous will want to experiment with other fruits and other herbs. This combination produces a fragrant, tasty pancake. (Shortcut: Use 1 cup biscuit mix in place of flour, baking powder, and oil.)

> 1 egg
> ½ cup milk, possibly more
> 2 tablespoons oil
> 1 cup sifted pastry or unbleached all-purpose flour
> 2 teaspoons baking powder
> 3 tablespoons sugar
> 1 large, ripe peach, finely chopped
> 3 teaspoons minced fresh savory, or 1 teaspoon ground
> Maple syrup or yogurt

1. Beat the egg, then add the milk and oil. Sift the flour with the baking powder and sugar into the egg mixture and stir just enough to blend. Add the chopped peach, including juice, and the savory. The batter should be easy to pour, and more milk may be added as needed.

2. Lightly grease a griddle or electric skillet, heat, and pour the batter in ¼-cup amounts to make small pancakes. Flip when bubbles circle the pancakes, and serve with maple syrup or a dollop of yogurt.

8–10 PANCAKES

Scottish Scones

Tea in the British Isles means scones, one of the most delicious members of the bread family. Try these rich ones with a dollop of whipped cream — clotted cream is hard to come by in the United States — and some strawberry jam.

1¾ cups unbleached all-purpose flour
4 tablespoons sugar
2½ teaspoons baking powder
½ teaspoon salt
1½ teaspoons minced fresh lemon thyme
⅓ cup butter
2 eggs
½ cup raisins, chopped
4–6 tablespoons light cream

1. Preheat the oven to 400°F. Combine the flour, sugar, baking powder, salt, and lemon thyme in the bowl of a food processor. Blend in the butter until the mixture looks like fine crumbs. Do not overmix.
2. In a large bowl, beat one egg and add the flour mixture. Stir in the raisins and enough of the cream so that the dough forms a ball. Turn the dough onto a lightly floured surface and knead about 10 times. Roll out to ½-inch thickness.
3. Beat the other egg. Cut the dough into circles with a biscuit cutter (2–2½ inches), place the circles on an ungreased cookie sheet, and brush with the beaten egg. Bake for 10–12 minutes or until golden brown. Immediately remove to a wire rack to cool, or serve warm.

10–12 SCONES

Thyme, from the Greek word for courage,
was said to invigorate warriors.

Sausage Bread

This puts the taste of a sandwich, delicately, into a slice of crusty, flavorful bread. It's done by machine, so just prepare the ingredients, pop them into the container, and let technology take it from there.

¼ pound hot Italian sausage, casing removed
1 large shallot (all the cloves)
1 teaspoon minced fresh thyme
1 teaspoon minced fresh parsley
1 teaspoon minced fresh marjoram
1 teaspoon minced fresh rosemary
¼ cup wheat bran
2 cups unbleached all-purpose flour
½ packet active dry yeast (1½ teaspoons)
1 tablespoon sugar
1 teaspoon salt
1 tablespoon grated cheese, mixed Parmesan and Romano
¾ cup water

1. Crumble or finely chop the sausage into a nonstick pan. Peel and chop the shallot.
2. Cook the sausage, continuing to separate any lumps. After a minute or two, add the shallot and herbs. Cook until the shallot is soft but not browned, then set the mixture aside to cool.
3. Using the order prescribed by your bread machine instructions, put the meat mixture along with the bran, flour, yeast, sugar, salt, cheese, and water into the machine. Process as basic bread.

1 SMALL LOAF

NOTE: *If you don't have a bread machine, you can make this recipe by adapting the instructions for the Herbed Focaccia or another yeast bread to fit these ingredients.*

Savory Onion Bread

The aroma of onion and garlic is mouthwatering. This bread has both, plus an assortment of other flavors that make it hard to wait for the oven to finish its work.

5 cups unbleached all-purpose flour
1 tablespoon sugar
½ tablespoon salt
1 packet active dry yeast
   (about 1 tablespoon)
1¼ cups milk
1 stick plus ⅔ stick butter, softened

2 eggs
3 garlic cloves, pressed
2 teaspoons minced sweet onion
3 teaspoons minced fresh savory
1 teaspoon caraway or sesame seeds
Freshly ground pepper
½ teaspoon hot sauce

1. In a large mixing bowl, combine 2 cups of the flour with the sugar, salt, and yeast.
2. Heat the milk with the ⅔ stick butter until warm.
3. Beat the eggs and add to the flour mixture, then add the milk mixture. Beat with an electric mixer on low until the flour is moist, then increase the speed to high and beat for 2 minutes.
4. Using your hands, blend in the rest of the flour. Turn the dough out on a lightly floured surface and knead. Butter the inside of the bowl and return the dough to the bowl, turning it until the surface is entirely covered with butter. Cover and put in a warm place until the dough rises to double its original bulk.

5. In the meantime, cream the full stick of butter with the garlic, onion, savory, caraway or sesame seeds, pepper to taste, and hot sauce.

6. Punch down the dough when it is ready, remove from the bowl, and divide in half. Roll one half into an 8 x 14-inch rectangle and spread half the seasoned butter over the dough. Roll up the rectangle and pinch the edges so that it closes tightly. Tuck the ends under and place in a greased or nonstick 4 x 8-inch loaf pan. Repeat for with other half. Cover both loaves with wax paper and let rise until the dough reaches the top of the pan.

7. Place the bread in an oven preheated to 350°F. Bake for 45 minutes or until a toothpick inserted in the center of each loaf comes out clean. Cool on metal racks.

2 LOAVES

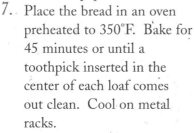

Herbed Focaccia

Focaccia used to be a rustic bread found all over Italy. Now it's a sophisticated bread found all over America.

> 1 packet active dry yeast (about 1 tablespoon)
> 1⅓ cups warm water
> 1 tablespoon extra virgin olive oil, plus more for oiling
> Salt
> 1¼ tablespoons minced fresh oregano
> 1¼ tablespoons minced fresh rosemary
> 1 tablespoon sun-dried tomatoes, packed in oil and drained
> 1½ cups whole wheat flour
> 1 to 1½ cups unbleached all-purpose flour

1. In a large bowl, dissolve the yeast in the water. Add the tablespoon of olive oil, salt to taste, 1 tablespoon of the oregano, 1 tablespoon of the rosemary, and the sun-dried tomatoes.
2. Stir in the whole wheat flour a half-cup at a time, beating until well blended. Stir in the all-purpose flour a half cup at a time until the mixture forms a ball.
3. Knead on a lightly floured surface for 10 minutes or until the dough is smooth and elastic. Form into a ball, place in an oiled bowl, and turn to cover the whole surface with oil.

4. Cover with a damp dish towel and let rise for 1–2 hours, or until it doubles in bulk. Punch down and knead a few times. Coat a 10-inch pie pan or 12-inch pizza pan with vegetable cooking spray and pat or roll the dough to fit the pan. Cover with a damp towel and let rise another 30 minutes.
5. Brush the dough with olive oil and scatter the remaining oregano and rosemary over the surface. In a preheated, 400°F oven, bake the focaccia for 25 minutes. Mist with water a few times during the first 15 minutes.
6. Cool on a rack. Serve warm or at room temperature.

1 LOAF

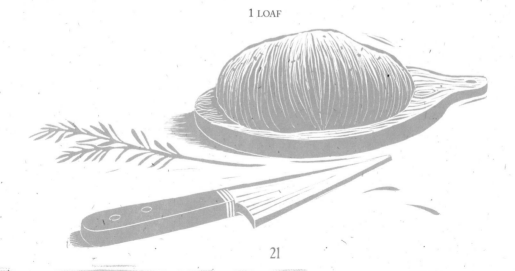

Grissini with Herbs

Bread sticks must be a first cousin to potato chips: It's hard to eat just one. These are crunchy through and through if you cook them 25 minutes, a bit softer at 20 minutes. Crispness also depends on how thinly they are rolled. The recipe makes four dozen, but they won't last long.

1 packet active dry yeast (about 1 tablespoon)	2¼ cups unbleached all-purpose flour
⅔ cup warm water	½ teaspoon white pepper
¼ cup extra virgin olive oil	1 tablespoon minced fresh rosemary
1 teaspoon salt	1 tablespoon minced fresh sage
1 tablespoon brown sugar	1 tablespoon minced fresh thyme
	1 egg, beaten

1. In a large bowl, stir the yeast into the water and set aside for 4 minutes. Pour in the olive oil, salt, brown sugar, and 1 cup of the flour and beat about 100 strokes. The dough will be smooth but sticky.
2. Gradually add more flour until the dough is soft. If it is still wet, add more.
3. On a lightly floured surface, knead the dough until it is smooth and elastic. Place in the bowl, cover with plastic wrap, and put in a warm place to rise until it doubles in bulk (about 1½ hours).
4. Punch down the dough and split it in half. Shape each half like a little loaf, cut down the middle lengthwise with a sharp knife, and keep dividing the

pieces in half until you have 24. It doesn't matter whether they are all the same size or not. Repeat with the other loaf.

5. Mix the pepper with the herbs and spread the mixture on a piece of wax paper. Press the cut side of a dough stick into the herbs and then roll it out on a board with your fingers, spreading it into a pencil-sized shape. Place the "pencils" on a greased or nonstick cookie sheet about ½ inch apart, brush with the beaten egg, and cover with slightly oiled wax paper that does not actually touch the dough. Let rise a second time until they have nearly doubled in bulk (30 to 40 minutes).

6. Preheat the oven to 325°F, remove the paper, and bake until the sticks are golden brown.

7. Cool the bread sticks on a rack and store in an airtight container. They can be frozen.

4 DOZEN BREADSTICKS

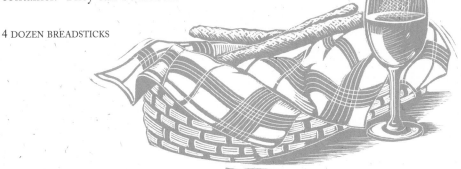

Black Bread

The dark loaves found in Hungary, Ukraine, and Russia have a hearty, peasant quality. Here's one made darker with instant coffee and flavored with caraway seeds.

2 packets active dry yeast
  (about 2 tablespoons)
¼ cup warm water
¼ cup plus 1 tablespoon yellow
  cornmeal
¾ cup cold water
¾ cup boiling water

1 tablespoon salad oil, plus more
  for oiling
2 teaspoons salt
4 tablespoons molasses
1½ teaspoons caraway seeds
2 tablespoons plus 1 teaspoon
  instant coffee
1 cup wheat bran
2 cups rye flour
2 cups unbleached all-purpose flour

1. Dissolve the yeast in the warm water and set aside.
2. Add the cornmeal to the cold water and mix well. Pour the boiling water into a large bowl and add the cornmeal mixture, stirring until thick. Stir in the oil, salt, molasses, caraway seeds, and 2 tablespoons of the instant coffee.
3. Add the yeast mixture and blend in the wheat bran and flours, adding more water if needed. Stir. The dough should be fairly sticky.
4. Turn onto a lightly floured surface and knead, adding flour as necessary, until you have a firm, elastic dough. Place in an oiled bowl, turning it to grease the dough on all sides. Cover with a damp dish towel and let rise in a warm place until about double in bulk, about 1½ hours.
5. Punch down the dough, knead 2 or 3 minutes more on a lightly floured surface, and then divide in half. Shape the two halves into free-form ovals, cover with a damp dish towel, and let rise again until almost doubled in bulk, about 30 minutes.
6. Preheat the oven to 400°F. Mix the remaining teaspoon of instant coffee with hot water and brush the loaves. Place them on a greased baking sheet and bake for 40–45 minutes, or until the bread sounds hollow when tapped. Cool on a wire rack.

2 LOAVES

Cheese Dilly Bread

In word association, dill goes with pickles. But it has a wider world. For centuries in the Middle East, dill has had medicinal value. In cooking, it appears with potatoes, fish, and eggs, and is one of the ingredients in curry powder. Here, it takes to bread.

3 cups unbleached all-purpose flour
1 cup whole-wheat flour
1 tablespoon baking powder
1 teaspoon salt
2 tablespoons snipped fresh dill weed
½ teaspoon celery seeds
Freshly ground pepper
1½ cups shredded Monterey Jack cheese
1 small onion, finely chopped (⅓ cup)
1 egg
1¾ cups buttermilk

1. Preheat the oven to 375°F. Grease two 4 x 8-inch pans and set aside.
2. In a large bowl, combine the flours, baking powder, salt, dill, celery seeds, pepper to taste, cheese, and onion.

3. In another bowl, mix the egg and buttermilk and add to the dry ingredients, stirring just enough to combine.
4. Spoon the batter into the two pans and bake until a toothpick inserted in the center comes out clean (35 to 40 minutes). Cool in the pans for 10 minutes, then on a rack.

2 LOAVES

Potato Bread with Chives

Make mashed potatoes without the usual flavorings, and then make this bread — a solid loaf that toasts well and tastes good.

½ *pound white potatoes (about 1 cup mashed)*
1 *cup potato water*
2 *packets active dry yeast (about 2 tablespoons)*
2 *tablespoons sugar*
2 *cups milk, warmed to the scalding point and cooled*
3 *tablespoons safflower or canola oil, plus more for oiling*
3 *teaspoons salt*
8 *cups unbleached all-purpose flour*
2 *tablespoons caraway seeds*
3 *tablespoons finely snipped fresh chives*

1. Peel and boil the potatoes until tender. Drain, reserving a cup of the cooking water, and mash the potatoes. Set aside to cool.
2. Dissolve the yeast in the tepid potato water and let stand about 3 minutes. Add the mashed potatoes, sugar, milk, oil, salt, and 4 cups of the flour. Beat until smooth.
3. Add the caraway seeds and the rest of the flour, or as much as is needed to make a fairly stiff dough.
4. Sprinkle the chives over the dough. On a lightly floured surface, knead until it is smooth and elastic, at least 10 minutes. Place in an oiled bowl, turning to coat the dough on all sides, and let rise until doubled in bulk (about an hour).
5. Punch down the dough, knead a few times, and shape or braid into three loaves. Place in greased pans and let rise again until double in bulk.
6. Preheat the oven to 350°F. Bake for 40 minutes.

3 LOAVES

Chives have been a favorite herb in the Orient
for over 3,000 years.

Bread Bouquet Garni

Aromatic in the kitchen, tasty on the tongue, this bread contains a potpourri of herbs. If you happen to be missing one of them, substitute a favorite or double one of those listed. This is one for the bread machine and produces a large loaf.

¼ cup wheat bran
¼ cup rolled oats
2½ cups unbleached all-purpose bread flour
2 tablespoons powdered buttermilk
1 cup plus 2 tablespoons water
1 egg
2 tablespoons butter
½ teaspoon salt
½ teaspoon brown sugar
1 teaspoon minced fresh marjoram
1 teaspoon minced fresh thyme
1 teaspoon minced fresh rosemary
1 teaspoon minced fresh parsley
1 teaspoon freshly ground black pepper
Slightly less than 1 packet active dry yeast (2½ teaspoons)

1. Combine the wheat bran, rolled oats, bread flour, and buttermilk.
2. Place ingredients in your bread machine in the order prescribed by the instruction book.

1 LARGE LOAF

NOTE: *If you don't have a bread machine, you can certainly knead this combination of herbs into your favorite white or sourdough bread.*

Fruity Bread with Thyme

Lots of breads are called quick breads. This one is speed demon bread. It takes a half hour from start to finish because the cooking is done in the microwave.

      2 cups sugar
    1½ cups safflower or canola oil
      3 eggs
      1 teaspoon vanilla
      2 cups fresh raspberries, mashed
      1 tablespoon chopped fresh thyme
      1 cup almonds, finely chopped
      3 cups unbleached all-purpose flour
      1 teaspoon salt
      1 teaspoon baking soda
      ½ teaspoon nutmeg

1. Grease two 4 x 8-inch glass or microwave-safe loaf pans and set aside.
2. In a large mixing bowl, beat the sugar, oil, eggs, and vanilla.
3. Add the raspberries, thyme, and half the almonds.
4. Stir in the flour, salt, baking soda, and nutmeg. Divide the batter between the two pans. Sprinkle with the remainder of the chopped almonds.
5. Cover with wax paper and microwave one loaf at a time for 10 minutes at the 5 or half-power setting, then another 2 minutes at full power. When a toothpick inserted in the center comes out clean, the loaf is done.

2 LOAVES

Oats and Prunes Bread

Healthy is how this bread sounds. But it's good, too. Since it seems like a breakfast food, it's nice to know that it makes excellent toast.

2 cups pitted prunes, cut in thirds
½ cup orange juice
1 cup unbleached all-purpose flour
1 cup whole wheat flour
¾ cup rolled oats
¼ cup wheat bran
½ cup granulated sugar
¼ cup brown sugar
1 tablespoon baking powder
¼ teaspoon salt
½ teaspoon cinnamon
2 teaspoons minced fresh thyme
¾ cup buttermilk
2 eggs
¼ cup safflower or canola oil

1. Preheat the oven to 350°F. Combine the prunes with the orange juice and let soak while preparing the rest of the ingredients. Grease two 4 x 8-inch loaf pans and set aside.
2. In a large bowl, combine the flours, oats, wheat bran, sugars, baking powder, salt, cinnamon, and thyme.
3. In a second bowl, blend the buttermilk, eggs, and oil. Quickly stir the liquid mixture into the dry ingredients. Add the prunes and orange juice mixture and stir. Spoon the batter into the pans.
4. Bake for 40–45 minutes or until a toothpick inserted in the center comes out clean. Cool for 10 minutes in the pans, remove, and finish cooling on a rack.

2 LOAVES

Banana Lemon Balm Bread

When your child says "Are these rotten enough?" in the supermarket, you just hope the world knows you're getting ready to make banana bread. Of course, they're not actually rotten, but the bananas need to be painfully close to create a mellow banana bread.

 1¾ cups unbleached all-purpose flour
 ¼ cup whole wheat flour
 1 teaspoon baking soda
 ½ teaspoon salt
 4 tablespoons butter, softened to room temperature
 ½ cup granulated sugar
 ½ cup light brown sugar
 2 eggs, beaten
 3 very ripe medium bananas
 1 teaspoon minced fresh lemon balm
 ⅓ cup milk

1. Preheat the oven to 350°F. Butter a 4 x 8-inch loaf pan and line with wax paper.
2. Sift together the flours, baking soda, and salt.

3. In a large bowl, cream the butter and sugars together. Blend in the eggs, bananas, and lemon balm. Add half the flour mixture and half the milk, stirring. Add the rest of the milk and then the rest of the flour mixture, and blend well. Pour into the loaf pan.
4. Bake for an hour or until a toothpick inserted in the center comes out clean.

1 LOAF

Minted Apple Bread

Like most quick breads, this one freezes well. Applesauce gives it moisture, spearmint gives it tang.

> 2 cups unbleached all-purpose flour
> ¾ cup brown sugar
> 1 tablespoon baking powder
> ½ teaspoon baking soda
> ½ teaspoon salt
> 1 teaspoon cinnamon
> 2 tablespoons minced spearmint
> 1 egg
> 1 cup unsweetened applesauce
> ¼ cup safflower or canola oil

1. Preheat the oven to 350°F. Grease two 4 x 8-inch loaf pans and set aside.
2. In a large bowl, combine the flour, brown sugar, baking powder, baking soda, salt, and cinnamon.
3. In a small bowl, stir together the spearmint, egg, applesauce, and oil. Add to the dry ingredients. Stir until blended. Pour batter into loaf pans and bake for 45 minutes or until a toothpick inserted in the center comes out clean.

2 LOAVES

Spearmint, also known as "lamb mint," "pea mint," and "garden mint," is the most used mint for culinary purposes.

Parsley Pine Nut Loaf

Pine nuts — pignolia in Italian — are sweet and crunchy. Added to this bread, along with fresh basil and parsley, they create a moist loaf that goes perfectly with a bowl of tomato soup.

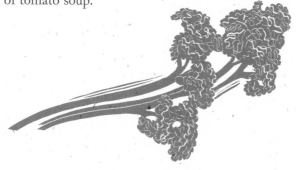

3 cups unbleached all-purpose flour
1 medium white onion, minced
   (about ¾ cup)
2 tablespoons sugar
4 teaspoons baking powder
½ teaspoon baking soda
½ teaspoon salt
⅓ cup extra virgin olive oil

1 cup milk
2 eggs
1 tablespoon minced fresh basil
1 tablespoon minced fresh parsley
1 tablespoon grated Romano cheese
¾ cup peeled and grated zucchini
½ cup pine nuts, slightly chopped

1. Preheat the oven to 350°F. Grease two 4 x 8-inch loaf pans.
2. In a large bowl, combine the flour, onion, sugar, baking powder, baking soda, and salt. In another bowl, whisk the oil, milk, eggs, herbs, and cheese. Add the zucchini and pine nuts.
3. Stir the liquid mixture into the flour mixture, and then spoon the batter into the pans. Bake for 45 minutes or until a toothpick inserted in the center comes out clean. Cool for 10 minutes before removing from pans.

2 LOAVES

In the language of flowers, parsley stands for festivity, while basil represents good wishes.

Country Bread

Dried sage may have created a harsh memory, but fresh sage delights the palate. Here it combines well with several kinds of flour for a peasant-style bread.

> 1 cup unbleached all-purpose flour
> ¼ cup whole wheat flour
> ½ cup cornmeal
> 2 tablespoons finely chopped fresh sage
> 2 teaspoons baking powder
> ½ teaspoon salt
> Freshly ground pepper
> 1 garlic clove, pressed
> ¼ cup olive oil
> 1 egg
> ½ cup buttermilk
> ¼ cup white wine

1. Preheat the oven to 350°F. Grease a shallow casserole or deep dish pie plate and set aside.
2. Combine the flours, cornmeal, sage, baking powder, salt, and pepper to taste.
3. Separately, whisk together the garlic, oil, egg, buttermilk, and wine. Fold the liquid mixture into the dry mixture and stir until combined.
4. Pour the batter into the casserole or pie plate and bake for 45 minutes or until a toothpick inserted in the center comes out clean. Cool for 10 minutes before removing from casserole.

1 LOAF

Sage was once believed to bestow immortality.

Pesto Roll

Basil came into its own when Americans began to substitute fresh green pesto sauce for the traditional red tomato sauce on their pasta. Now pesto goes into soups, onto pizza, or atop polenta. Here, it's rolled up inside a delicious eggy bread.

THE PESTO
½ cup olive oil
¼ cup grated Romano and Parmesan cheese
2 tablespoons pine nuts
1 cup basil leaves
1 cup parsley, stems removed
Juice of 1 lemon

FOR THE ROLL
4 tablespoons butter
½ cup unbleached all-purpose flour
2 cups milk
Salt and freshly ground pepper
5 eggs, separated

FOR THE FILLING
Pesto
2 cups ricotta cheese
2 tablespoons shredded
   mozzarella cheese

1. Combine all the pesto ingredients in a blender or food processor.
2. Preheat the oven to 400°F. Grease an 11 x 16-inch jelly roll pan, line with parchment paper, oil the paper, and sprinkle with flour.

3. Melt the butter in a saucepan, remove from the stove, and stir in the flour. Add the milk and cook until boiling, stirring constantly. Simmer for 2 minutes, then add salt and pepper to taste.
4. Beat in the egg yolks one at a time. Beat the egg whites until they stand in soft peaks; fold into the white sauce. Spread the mixture in the jelly roll pan. Bake for 30 minutes.
5. When the roll is done, turn it out on a clean dish towel on a flat surface. To add the filling, spread the roll with a layer of pesto followed by an extra layer of ricotta. Starting on the long side, roll the whole thing up. Sprinkle with shredded mozzarella and return to the oven to keep warm and to melt the cheese. Cut into thick slices.

6 SERVINGS

Delicious Dumplings

Call them gnocchi in Italy or spaetzle in Germany, European dumplings come in a variety of shapes and sizes. These are Eastern European and are perfect in chicken soup or with a cream gravy.

6 *shallots, minced (3 tablespoons)*
3 *tablespoons butter*
3½ *cups cubed white bread, crusts removed*
2 *eggs*
¾ *cup milk*
2 *tablespoons finely chopped parsley*
½ *teaspoon salt*
2 *cups unbleached all-purpose flour*

1. Cook the shallots in the butter until golden and soft. Add the bread cubes and cook until they start to brown. Cool.
2. In a large bowl, combine the eggs, milk, parsley, and salt. Stir in the bread and shallots mixture and let stand for 5 minutes.
3. Stir in enough of the flour to make a soft, slightly sticky dough. In a soup pot, heat about 2 quarts of water to a boil. With flour-covered fingers, shape the dough into 1-inch balls and drop, one at a time, into the boiling water.

4. Simmer uncovered until the dumplings rise to the surface, stirring occasionally to make sure none are stuck to the pot. Simmer another 6 minutes. Remove the dumplings with a slotted spoon or Chinese strainer.

25–30 ONE-INCH DUMPLINGS

Cranberry Fritters

Like French cheeses, fritters seem to stake out regional territories. Some places you find them with clams, other places with corn. Here the deep-fried delectables come with cranberries for tartness and rosemary for fragrance.

> 2 cups raw cranberries
> 2 eggs
> 6 tablespoons honey
> 2 tablespoons melted unsalted butter
> 2 teaspoons orange zest
> 2 teaspoons minced fresh rosemary leaves
> 1¼ cups unbleached all-purpose flour
> ¼ teaspoon salt
> 2 teaspoons baking powder
> Powdered sugar for topping

1. Wash, sort, and coarsely chop the cranberries. Cook in water to cover until just soft — they'll start to pop at that point. Drain well and spread out on paper towels.
2. In a large bowl, beat the eggs, add the honey, and continue beating. Beat in the butter, orange zest, and rosemary. Stir in the cranberries.

3. Sift the flour, salt, and baking powder together. Add to the cranberry mixture and blend gently.
4. Drop the batter from a teaspoon into deep fat that has been preheated to between 350°F and 365°F. Use a candy thermometer to maintain the right temperature.
5. Fry a few fritters at a time until they are golden brown, about 3–4 minutes. Remove with a slotted spoon and drain on paper towels.
6. Test the first few fritters to make sure they are moist but not runny. Sift powdered sugar over them and serve warm. They will keep in a low oven for a while, if necessary.

ABOUT 18 FRITTERS

Apple Sage Stuffing

The aroma of Thanksgiving, hours before dinner is served, holds people hostage, not only on the holiday itself but in memory as well. Early in the morning, the stuffing gets the holiday started, sending a smell of butter, garlic, and onions through the house. Here's one way to fill up the turkey cavity and wake the hungry.

6 tablespoons butter
1 stalk celery with leaves, chopped (about ½ cup)
2 garlic cloves, mashed
2 medium onions, chopped (about 1 cup)
1 large apple, peeled and chopped (about 1 cup)
4 cups bread cubes
1 cup hot water
2 eggs, beaten
1 tablespoon minced fresh sage
1 tablespoon minced fresh thyme
1 teaspoon salt
Freshly ground pepper

1. In a deep skillet, melt the butter and sauté the celery, garlic, and onions until soft but not browned. Add the apple and stir for about 2 minutes.
2. Remove from heat. In a large bowl, combine the apple mixture with the bread cubes, hot water, eggs, sage, and thyme.
3. Stir until well blended, adding more hot water if needed. The stuffing should be moist but not wet. Add the salt and the pepper to taste.

ENOUGH STUFFING FOR A 14-POUND TURKEY

Zucchini Cornbread

When you are overwhelmed with zucchini and underwhelmed with ideas, this recipe will help use up quite a few of the infamous green summer squash. If they've hidden under the vines and gotten big enough to make a dugout canoe, don't despair — peel off the tough skin and grate the rest.

3 or 4 *zucchinis, grated (about 6 cups)*
2 *teaspoons salt*
2 *cups cornmeal*
1 *cup unbleached all-purpose flour*
1 *tablespoon baking powder*
3 *eggs, beaten*
2 *tablespoons honey*
1½ *cups buttermilk*
2 *tablespoons minced fresh oregano*

1. Preheat the oven to 350°F. Place the zucchini in a colander and toss with 1 teaspoon of the salt to draw out some of the liquid. Let drain about 30 minutes.
2. Sift together the cornmeal, flour, baking powder, and the rest of the salt.
3. Mix the eggs, honey, buttermilk, and oregano. Combine with the dry ingredients.

4. Rinse the salt from the zucchini and squeeze out the water. You will have about 3 cups of pulp. Stir into the batter.
5. Pour the batter into a 9-inch springform pan or two small loaf pans, and bake for 40 minutes. Cool for about 10 minutes before removing from pans.

8–10 SERVINGS

Quesadillas with Tortillas de Harina

Quesadillas can be lunch or surprising hors d'oeuvres. Tortillas can be purchased in most groceries, but they can also be made at home. These are the flour tortillas of Mexico — soft and nearly white. Many Mexican women still pat them into rounds with their hands, but they can also be made with a tortilla press — or just rolled with a rolling pin.

TORTILLA INGREDIENTS
- 4 cups unbleached all-purpose flour
- 2 teaspoons salt
- ⅓ cup shortening
- 1 cup warm water

1. Sift the flour and salt together and work the shortening in with the fingertips or blend it quickly in a food processor, being careful not to overblend. Stir in enough water to form a firm ball, adding extra if needed. Knead well.
2. Form balls about the size of an egg, and roll between well-oiled sheets of wax paper into 8-inch circles. The tortillas should be fairly thin. Cook on a medium-hot griddle, 2 minutes on the first side and only a minute on the second.

Quesadilla filling

- 1 cup shredded Monterey Jack cheese
- 1 cup shredded sharp cheddar cheese
- 2 tomatoes, seeded, drained, and diced
- 2 tablespoons chopped fresh oregano
- 4 tablespoons chopped fresh parsley
- 1 teaspoon cumin

1. Place a flour tortilla on a cookie sheet. Scatter some cheese, tomatoes, oregano, parsley, and cumin on it, staying a quarter inch away from the edge. Put another tortilla on top, and repeat the layer of cheese, tomatoes, and herbs. Top with a third tortilla.

2. Repeat the process with three more tortillas until all the ingredients have been used. Bake in a 400°F oven for 6–8 minutes. Cut into pie-shaped pieces and serve hot.

AT LEAST 3 STACKS, 6–8 PIECES EACH

Bruschetta

When you soak your fresh Italian bread in olive oil laced with garlic, you're partaking not only of a tempting appetizer but of a centuries-old practice. In ancient Rome, the first taste of freshly pressed, green olive oil was via an oil-soaked piece of bread. In recent years, bruschetta has become fashionable in better Italian restaurants. Here's a version you can try for yourself.

8 slices of Italian bread
4 large garlic cloves, peeled and sliced in half
½ cup olive oil, as green as possible
1 teaspoon freshly ground pepper

1. Toast the bread.
2. While it is hot, rub one side with garlic.
3. Serve the toast garlic side up, with olive oil on the side. Guests can spoon olive oil over their toast slices, add a couple of twists of the pepper grinder, and enjoy being with-it — and with the centuries.

4 SERVINGS

Catalan Classic

Thousands of Americans had their first taste of tomato bread at the 1992 Olympic Games in Barcelona, center of Spain's Catalan culture. It is simple but seductive.

1 loaf crusty bread, cut in half lengthwise
3–4 garlic cloves, sliced in half
4 ripe tomatoes
Spanish olive oil
Salt
Sweet white onion for garnish (optional)
Pitted black olives for garnish (optional)

1. Rub the cut side of the bread with the garlic cloves, then cut each half crosswise into inch-thick pieces. Brown the bread under the broiler, being careful not to burn it.
2. Cut the tomatoes in half and rub the toasted bread with the tomato, letting the pulp sink in. Discard the skin. Dribble olive oil over the tomato bread and sprinkle lightly with salt to taste.
3. Serve immediately as is, or garnish with a slice of onion and an olive.

4–6 SERVINGS

Sesame Rounds

It may seem absurd — given all the variety available at the supermarket — to make crackers, but it's not. Try these and see.

> 1 cup sesame seeds
> 2 cups unbleached all-purpose flour
> 1 teaspoon salt
> Dash cayenne
> 12 tablespoons butter
> ¼ cup ice water
> 1 tablespoon minced fresh parsley, washed and dried

1. Preheat the oven to 300°F. In a dry skillet, brown the sesame seeds, stirring so they don't burn.
2. In a bowl, combine the flour, salt, and cayenne. Cut in the butter. Add the ice water a tablespoon at a time. Add the sesame seeds.
3. Roll the dough to ¼-inch thickness. Sprinkle evenly with the parsley and give it another quick roll. Cut into small rounds, 1½ inches across. Bake 30 minutes or until lightly brown.
4. Cool on a rack and store in a tightly closed container.

24 CRACKERS

Provence Spread

Top quality olive oil is the ticket here. Don't look at the unit price, just keep tasting until you find a fine olive oil that you like. Some chefs swear by Spanish olive oil, others only use Italian. Saying they are all alike is like saying all potatoes are the same.

½ cup pitted black olives
½ cup pitted green olives
¾ cup extra virgin olive oil
6 garlic cloves
2 tablespoons capers
Juice of ½ small lemon (2 teaspoons)
Salt and freshly ground pepper
Crusty Italian or French bread

1. Finely chop enough black olives to make 1 tablespoon. Do the same with the green, mix the two, and set aside.
2. Pour the oil into a blender and add the garlic, capers, and lemon juice. Blend until almost smooth.
3. Put the oil mixture into a small bowl and stir in the chopped olives. Add salt and pepper to taste.
4. Spread on thin slices of toast made with crusty bread.

1 CUP

Herb Cheese Spread

Cooks usually want their families to wait until fresh loaves of bread cool before they are cut. But everyone knows a warm loaf melts the butter — or this cheesy mix. Try it on a crusty heel of whole wheat or oatmeal, five minutes out of the oven.

8 tablespoons butter, softened
3 cups grated cheddar cheese
2 tablespoons finely snipped fresh chives
1 tablespoon caraway seeds
2 tablespoons cognac

1. Beat the butter and cheese together.
2. Blend in the chives, caraway seeds, and cognac.

ABOUT 2 CUPS

Mustard Spread

Add a little spice to bread or crackers with this smooth, herbed spread.

> 8 *tablespoons butter, softened*
> 1 *tablespoon finely chopped fresh parsley*
> 1 *tablespoon finely chopped fresh basil*
> 1 *tablespoon spicy mustard*
> *Bread or crackers*

1. Using an electric mixer or a food processor, cream the ingredients together.
2. Spread on bread or crackers. It will keep in the refrigerator for several weeks.

ABOUT ½ CUP

Index

Converting Recipe Measurements to Metric

Use the following formulas for converting U.S. measurements to metric. Since the conversions are not exact, it's important to convert the measurements for all of the ingredients to maintain the same proportions as the original recipe.

WHEN THE MEASUREMENT GIVEN IS	MULTIPLY IT BY	TO CONVERT TO
teaspoons	4.93	milliliters
tablespoons	14.79	milliliters
fluid ounces	29.57	milliliters
cups (liquid)	236.59	milliliters
cups (liquid)	.236	liters
cups (dry)	275.31	milliliters
cups (dry)	.275	liters
pints (liquid)	473.18	milliliters
pints (liquid)	.473	liters
pints (dry)	550.61	milliliters
pints (dry)	.551	liters
quarts (liquid)	946.36	milliliters
quarts (liquid)	.946	liters
quarts (dry)	1101.22	milliliters
quarts (dry)	1.101	liters
gallons	3.785	liters
ounces	28.35	grams
pounds	.454	kilograms
inches	2.54	centimeters
degrees Fahrenheit	$^5/_9$ (temperature − 32)	degrees Celsius

While standard metric measurements for dry ingredients are given as units of mass, U.S. measurements are given as units of volume. Therefore, the conversions listed above for dry ingredients are given in the metric equivalent of volume.